MOB

Also by Abigail Child

From Solids (Segue, 1983)
Climate/Plus (Coincidence Press, 1986)
A Motive for Mayhem (Potes & Poets Press, 1989)
Flash (Zet, 1990)

MOB

ABIGAIL CHILD

O Books
Oakland, CA

ACKNOWLEDGEMENTS

Thanks to the editors of the following magazines in which versions of these works appeared: *WRITING, MIRAGE #4/Period(ical), RADDLE MOON, BIG ALLIS, DEAR WORLD, MOTEL, 6IX, CHAIN* and *THE ART OF PRACTICE: Forty-Five Contemporary Poets;* and to Kevin Davies and Carla Harryman for their supportive readings and suggestions. Phrases from Andy Levy's *Rumi Improvisations* and Diane Ward's *Crossing* are used in *Beyond Surplus* with appreciation.

Cover photo by Arthur Fellig (Weegee) "Coney Island, 28th of July, 1940, 4 'clock in the afternoon" by permission of the International Center of Photography, New York.

Typesetting by Annie Stenzel

Copyright © Abigail Child
Library of Congress No.94-067492
ISBN No.1-882022-21-1

O Books
5729 Clover Street
Oakland, CA 94618

Contents

MOB

Ballot	9
Crank	10
Pulse	11
Public Opinion	13
Lick	14
Bulge	15
Peel	16
Sail	17
Torque	18
Meld	19
Squeeze	20
Strap	21
Skate	27
Bolt	31
Flesh	33
Surplus	39

UNCHAINED REACTION	41
TWO COUNTRIES	53
CIVILIAN LIBERTY	61
BEYOND SURPLUS	73
LEGACY	83
RAPTURE	94

MOB

BALLOT

Upset plank fortified ousting
rowdy cock surrenders bludgeon
scarred modest kisses
face limit, fumble
in wracked clog
of jubilant status

Fright chills title
immortalizes habit
arc of the outlaw
continues
—longlining

A build-up at dawn
encounters no mercy
thumb oppositions
—no radical
—no safety

CRANK

Air buys in
intransient to butcher looks
disconcertingly funk
nonplussed

Tenor on slow
chewing doable ice
twork internal scrawl
Color dumb luck

We're muscle lust
encrusted deuce sucker
fuck

Predicated prefaces slam
imperfectly
my mongrel *my* timber my *mon*
titillated against congealed nuance

Below bobble dents
array A—
vital spot
alloy galore

Jumboized eye
eminently leapers

I just
I lust
shaped to retrieve

PULSE

At this moment the evidence of kisses behind her
assured quietly that stretch of russet in the exhausting flats
was not expectation turned round to gaze at its own light
but a future without hyperbole, without suffix,
with hesitations
the sky is drunk with

The center in front of the future
before embarrassment
reads borrowed warmth
no less for that

Light is our object. Our object orientation
would be naked feet of room.
A pedestal of this idea interrupted

Thus frames hit the screen
dependent on the intent
first in concept of light or of light and its glow
either no sound or sound completely filled

o

as if the smooth equivalent of a certain *contact*
had touched a civilization
or a civility had broken at last
inadequate in retrospect.

wants nothing more gruesome than the real

This mechanics, a material
system weighting the law.
The picture its own fathers and sons.

PUBLIC OPINION

Even the smokers pause between bites
disdain their gates
beardless in chronic screaming
will swarm your head

Fully automatic
just dropped, in all or some of today's too
short, who on hype
might seem appointed

A closed-circuit television
during the rally
tries to end the parties' play by play
unsanctioned on transfer

Brought to you by
the ideologically neutral
which include every man's
numb hands

To pay nothing
nothing
for the co-location in gradient tints
jeopardizing the correction

And plausibility of navigation's explosion
in piecemeal to perform
War
protrudes from categories

Earth
programmatically excluded
inverts this cliché
of *something forever*

LICK

Meaning at this point
the heart is an exaggeration
increasingly insecure Americans
use

To arrive at the figure they need
making need
the figure they want
to maintain a magnitude of death

Exploding alarms came down
echoing embryonic teletronic effect
can kill or maim
and you call it your job

BULGE

Immunology cuteness besieged now
picks fucks besmirches office
pitched ruin
hats

Executive realness hurts
screws
crisp magnetic cookies
(overcooked)

Compulsion balks
harnessed by explosions
discrete signal throbs
the basis of makeup

Dampening kiss outlives utopia
compulsion outlives rancor
a charm responds
pitched at sleep

Bias meters handling still
translate stall
snap to terminal bruise
uncounted corners

Perpendicular blue
sky torn
unequally
awake

PEEL

I can't remember how to "get" the picture

Love sticks up
between mutuality
to make sense of
body

not as a rule but a break
in particular
just a lark to a fault

until repair is stalled

SAIL

Appealing id I'd rather
flutter in lecture cc's
sized by cold invade
lit glut
attested

Violation bride uncocked jocks
queue
"interpreted to death"
introjects
calibrated circumstance

Ripping big for it
raucous branches
double up
between us
Row bowed weirdly

Blunt whipping planet rout
under model dollar bus
routes upset rain
refuses slam
Lilacs tear

Large lips
put up a storm
round cutoffs
catches
to come apart

The head stays on

TORQUE

There
in the suburban darkness sweetly enveloped
in the most morbid security of day
a misnomer —
building in its thrilling way
the sense of entanglements, warnings and promise

that made us just a little hungry and *duded* for that purpose
hand-delivered—brain-lost—near-nuclear
potential in fact is broken
spreads
ignited on the imagination of love
A short high-pressure explosive without conclusion

Your hands are long-duration pressure pulses
where love takes over
this might not protect you
is insufficient, radical
opposed
to the assurance of a future

advancing behind you

MELD

Destitution pulleys control TV
woo women
speeded up
Life edits yes

I'll buy the heat

Flush of languor onto blonde lilt
wanting ream to string
and holing up
The vocabulary in my house

Wanting the outside in
and hearing severe design

She shielded that steely eye.

Hoping to negotiate
as if the delicate petition
someone penned
Would be assent.

*She realized mascara was a stimulant
for a face that never ran.*

Energy eyes pile up
until present day mutates
Amiss to relax the tongue
Comes apart

In caress
quivering knee resists
touches her mouth
Buffeted dumb

I want the whole essay

SQUEEZE

Adhesion to this body
muscle mouths consummator
so kinky in copyright
so lavish in orifice
so luck in my bit
gossamer topsided

Focusing argument
to penetrate asshole
sticky and stocky
stocky and plastic
beneath cuddling
embarrassment to represent

Sensible prisoners
across the playhead
deposit repeatedly,
longingly (re)call
—
clitoral high of my childhood

Impressed pulse
plays back alternate skins
to wick away wet
dicked by technique
Her red is illegal
she talks in her sleep

STRAP

The first word is *robbed*
then *backassed*
a sanitized American
downbeat
washing threat

Instead of CUNT ON COT GUN IN MOM O

I want a hibernator
as well as BAD BAD BAD
staccato

Nothing else is pinning it

On that edge
be done with them.

I wake up, I ream, I shock a quest
on kicks in French and realize
I can make a sentence

*The tree leaves of some street species
are going red*

I smell fresh exemption

a clutch of struts
not as full as suppose
unless there is
an affable whole
opened up

But there is never enough

Fullness become a light
to go around
agreement's control
disagreeing ground

He won't go to the dog

The world hangs up

should
better
but

We won't

tunnels
vault
balloon

wants want

dummies in their hands
with product display

a shot of their balls
summarizing power

What does ugly mean in a city of beggars?

Ghetto
binoculars
indifferently
list

indigenous
calumnies

All punishment embroiders comparison
Strap
wants to bite on the world
runs against

Why there is no vessel to hold it?

The understory made up of suppressed individuals
of the same overstory species

*I can't respond
which makes my body feel attacked by noise
and told to hide*

Exhilarate the vacuum

Rubberized American genitals perpetuate
her deprived transcendence

I keep an eye out the armpit
watch tents upended quietly
while plaintive pundits
ring useless rules

Nearer a rotted sun
the women emerge
shocked fetuses
locked-in-legs

The experiment insults everyone

Dead flesh

cut off from argue
crowded with gamma gamma reservation
tugger penis
paying swamp

The boy symbol become the poem
subordinating half-light suicides

The first realism becomes the Other

eluding the pressure
raided by absence

SKATE

Consider:
>Proportion belongs to the realm
>of stagecraft, fiction

>Desire making heads
>in the rest of the body
>yanked and jolted by reverse orgasm

I have told no one
>*a suspicion many have*
>*to do with anything that is*
>*happening to you to*
>*myself for you at the situation is*

to make a different decision

which reveals the molecular structure of your disbelief

You save us without rhythm

The belly surfaces
as concentrate and irrevocably in love
as to curves on if to come

A hold sign is counteracted
by specific leg gestures
which show that you leave the ground

I could be on top of you
loving the nape and breast of you
grinding the bone in voluptuous tending
in need with her line to conquer
(like a commercial movie Mom wouldn't go to)

smacks drags skewered blinds

This path can be broken up
with communications that the economic criteria of
language consider underdeveloped

I cannot

I cannot

I cannot

    (not like it)

Anguish humiliates me
Ampersand of symbolic corkscrew twists
making tissue spell anger

Reluctant silhouettes synthesizing punches
until you form a more
acceptable problem

Our still original slum is specifically
letter original

You take sex with a belt
with shape
with ring
with my eyes

and absorb the sensation
coveting it

slime softened
exhausted and lathered
Even lying can be indicated by using the starting position
It doesn't matter which Even is part of life, it annexes

The dirtiness remains repressed.

BOLT

Copulation read
as a successful restablishment of power
Discourse as defense
in a period of colonial expansion

The dream sequence is ambiguous:

Does the Asian get fucked?
                              mutual
buttocks and breasts
                              studied
                                                  nonchalance
gorgeous
                              oysters
                                                  held captive
inside my   pectoral

                suicide
                                  perverse
                                  butt
for spilling
                                                  the milk
                     indigenous

knocked out strictly

Now what have we here?

A jury circumvents interrogation
locking distraction
 in commodity ikons

industrial plumping
 a misleading orgasm

stung fun   transposed
in hulk
                of distaff
                              lingual

glozing

smoke
hole up

Die excellently.

FLESH

Romanticism betrays the animal line
in colonialism of closeup

I stand in front and manage the meeting
There's a skin game by a secret entrance
a well-paralleled penis with moving parts in the panel

The lead is a lion and a widow in the making
sprayed through holes
panting host plimsols pouncy pumps
at sun's galore
is a chalk or dust with fire shapes
functions to shake
be attention to stone
in silence
disintegrate

swarm

where we touch
this

Black trees go to sleep
colors engrave sensitivities
where we kiss
(link)
opposite angular expects
the congestion
we have still
of Ideal,
and chuck up
to start

Later
rag leaves go yellow
bumps struck cold
path filled with hung trees

The wind pushes it forward

o

You own the red in that pop
And consequently
I felt the warm shape of her vulva
peach blood
with common sense

(encircled by same red)

Love has dreaming
is never the same

Exemption hurts to dream
We sleep ourselves ironically
recurring faces
illuminate the overeaten fragments

Pressure pans backwards
up to speech
Your hands are lost
it drafts
until a great bounces up
INTERPOPS
dazzling final plays in the rips
of tumbled bodies and infinite
think

Wacky model
covered with mavericks
Lateral spin pillowed by nature
back through to nascent
to hotdog
to high heels
to type this:
his porcupine is a consummation
kite

Density mirrors
mapping molecules and shapes of
carry volunteers
to touch
inside the blue and black
and spit it out

Response of pause to place
to be your freedom's skin
splits small distances

Lender meats look blank
without scent react
full of inside surrounds

or laws we wish exempt

I catch the echo

The way the trees go red
Year
some bother
some forget

Shocking nature which isn't cool
arrives to stand
alas
EVEN as the arrogance of her conclusions' fury

mime panic opponents
that shadow that
in form of double yellow lines
to sky the equation

Not of rule but of succession
—stretched
as in the mechanical horse
or the arm you feel

The denial
this decision has caused

I want to drink the theory
wilting the interim

SURPLUS

While this kind of consolation and exhortation
is expensive
you you so merrily merrily swoon

The windows gather place
the mouth is grasped
manually

Behind the silver plate
someone hates (defective and ancient)
surrounded by camouflage escapes

That rudimentary alluring yet annoying
suburban, happy
protocol explodes

Machines turning phoney
more insidious, more common
birds appear anywhere

Flush twilight
startling the exception
knotted cords, bright quarters

The sun fulfills itself
makes no comparison

UNCHAINED REACTION

Rods act out

Read gold stars on a ceiling of excess

We conquer our freedom

And this everywhere throughout

The city fragrant in evening trees—

Russian olive, rose and plane

Together with murmur of crowds

Bodies in shadow

Space begun and limbs impersonal

Ikon rounds at century's end

A basket of cherubs above heads of the dying

Mute stares sublimated, ravished

Figure tumbles forward dismantling

Any frame to contain her

The shape clocked later

No thank you

On a flat beach studded with shoppers

I don't want encircled salvation

Sustained by routine

The elevator here and *do you need?*

A little stiff good fortune and shelter

Behind our lids your stroke laps

Margin in night promenade

Music boats pedal past tents

Colored to find your way home

In the ocean. Europe roots in America

Asks: *Where are the televisions?*

Screwing discovery of tongues

Passing over to you

Rather thin and dark under lit night piazza

Compressed explosion to renovate cinema

Or are they lovers? become a bathing

Suit of terminated xxx's. The body remains

Spectacular organized SPASMS

Still molten, instinct without

Which the entire waking of her consciousness

How can I make this irrational?

That is to say, belief is a privilege

Would you like to leave a message?

Only flesh is in color

Invading in consequence

Neither floating nor blooming

Hydraulic kinetics, a push-pull animal

The day, the days, the nights,

I come, I do not come

At the front or out back remains

Like a fire he assimilates

All the rest of the animals killed in his shadow

How do they do it?

The house is claustrophobic

The living body passes into use, becomes

Tool and demonstration

The furrow polluted below

This magnificent, uninterrupted contour

I write it myself It's picturesque

Sparked on next

Precious, locked in time, excessive

Gold, lamb, deer, peacock, dove

A promise transparent in empire's shift

Cut out on the map

A skeletal world of constructivist colonialisms

Seen through glass

Schooled beneath deceit and elaborate abstracts

Dinner is served deep blue, striped at top

Six persons and so many cyclists

Shall we stay here? offering up a flood

While the stream widens

Detaching hands

And a slow alteration spans years

Discontinuity does not mean break

The most inward push lips pull apart

Wind carries an odor

Loaded, reluctant

Sounds recast facts

I imagine our relation a tactical action

A vital discretion unstuck in the sense

Here is your condom

These brown or blue hatchings

A necessary refusal, entirely confessed

These blanks are annoying

One pulls the other by hand on top of a motor

At dusk white light cuts back to café

Stroll through economy mall replicates

Decorated cake of religion

Detail. Dust to empty

Time is stopped or forwarded

With whom am I talking?

I kiss her, *eye* cunning

Studded with dreams

Greater from this contact

They wade out in the ocean

Forgetting birth in a future *I am going there*

Materializing realities that we call size and duration

False constants, dispersion of objects

Energy in any language

Beyond locale *Let's go*

To catch within between

We have given life to earth by lending it

The pretense of our unity

Part of the problem: how to define relations

Glorious with pupils contracted from the day denied

And night an illusion taking place

In a current millennium *octopuslike*

How does it stay here and take the sun?

The water not cold. I speak, impend

There is no shortage

God the father *is* the commercial.

The stench underneath

Illusions of manure

Not unlike power

Surprised by penetration

English subtitles take to the street

Recasting the sheet

Which furls back into it

You are right. Counting the waves we

Begin to forget the tide.

Impelled by language sky

And earth disjoint. Verbs spring open

Unobliged

TWO COUNTRIES

Bodies coexist in motion

Sun low over Upjohn Chemical

    •

The field has more yellow
is sink white, bright white, iridescent
under a sky formed regionally and in jerks

    •

in perfect disagreement with the dictates of
War

In order to entirely satisfy, something must be
evaded

    •

Bombing scenarios on TV mark the failure of the physical

Trees have shadows, empirical stripes
massy, insistent

    •

still fresh, still climbing

    •

A "wet-dick party" is how he described it

-

      roping vowels
      on a double
      incline

-

Pushing the shape

rapid blossoming
light, against the background of stars
and movement of planets

drawn from the ears, tongue-tied,
snack-footed snow swept once
and patterned wastes of high volcanoes on a cycle platform

-

    I admit it's difficult. The lines are more numerous
       They intersect less and less often and further

wobbling stun
pedal initiative

   from us than we thought

-

   as if ,
   the month of days could make carved rocks
conditional

-

A victim of the sum
unreconciled 'midst mutual technology

Everything sweats
The colors go even. The light pales
The colors disappear. Everyone is huge

   •

and then we meet
a *norteamericano* "who knows how to do things"

   •

  So big he had a room for me to decorate

   •

  I defend my antagonist

T-shirt reads: *lick it suck it slam it*
and on the reverse a price list

16 billion 33 billion 300 billion
contaminates
washed up
  from Carwash Cenote

   •

  A body bag ends the list of oil products

   •

this landscape salty, poorer,
occupied

       Worker semiplex Worker pictures
       underemployed Worker

   •

       Can you make sense of this future?

   •

Wanting the biograph to be a first step in serial composition,
subject to hybridization

   •

slaves and honey *miel de abejas*
beneath "fierce" sun

   •

The man as objectified muscle tames the beast of burden
She rides the glamorously exotic circus elephant

    We get a canned version of some mass that remains
unnamed
      because there's too much break-up in this system

   •

       Extinguished night starts again
       lacunae exist.
           see: wetness

   •

Shadows heave irregular flowers

The empty and pockmarked.
The perfectly sporty
A Mayan nose
> *biologically*
> *Living beings hold together*

•

A man annihilated in black rains of flesh

True men are made from coincident beds

Become laminated, crumpled, crushed, prised loose

      Which is correct?

•

      a más cerca al último, tiene más calor

head whacks in reverse
Coca-Cola canned between lagoons

•

somewhat loosened
looking impressed
and roughened
      by money

•

vistas speak of a high-level conquest
enlarging the supporting mound

sun rakes stairs with handles of limestone

        ticking time
        shallow
        reedy
        burgeoning

    •

heat
under shadow of ruin

    •

A plan with built-in excavations

    •

    All the work in a sentence.

    •

    The pronoun matters only when excluded

    •

In parenthesis
unfolding breaker mimes earth in movement

    •

The present and past irradiate each other
Sky keeps time
enormous foam

    •

                    sea-tossed
                    in the margins

                        (stoney)

                •

The clouds are Hollywood
The foolish tourists sit in skulls surround
the backs of slaves on which a regal
            leader stands

            on the backs of slaves

                •

            and we stand under

                •

conquest with collateral distance

((as seen on TV))

                •

(permissable) in the act of blood-letting

"Taking" more to the point

Greed, and a kind of impossibly hard cruel horrifically
snouted façade
                •

            has fleshless jaws

                •

>   and his enemy "death"
>
>   collapsed bone

             •

When smoke clears, disturbances are forwarded.
They form a double ululation
festooned across an inner ear

                 •

marked in figures
consumed in transport

                 •

            Land invaded to leave no part of it in
light

             •

Infected occluded
   globe
begun again against an axis made

            fist

            raw

            uneven

CIVILIAN LIBERTY

landscape
haunts presumption
wearing an accumulation

Vocables reign over the night too angry, it's as No,
to get out in which this exists and why should they?
They deserve to stay. Limbs unduly, graven to incident, lit
phosphine, a woman doing it. This is the space of America's
future: insulted reflection to visceral soak. The machines
have harried the body. The police arrive. Sexual take
making minimal crush like odor doping lips spontaneously
flammable.

The shadows so fine they make lines on the pavement,
monuments
to the bodies' *get along*.

spectacle parries

A polished fragment

illegally alert

As the whole microcosm. *We just don't discuss that comparison.* The dialogue an echo of damage, media chapped more easily sullen. *You know how it gets fine through misfortune. You are more fortified with it— before it gets fine.* And he is fortunate to earn one dollar a day. Dandy baby, colorless phooey. Invasion sap, not us, structure the the original unfit fist of two coins. Measure. She is saying: *living is almost the art of life.* In a country in which the eight-hour day is a racial category it's bad luck: the privilege of a window ignoring its cost.

On top of whatever you are thinking the street keeps sounding. Mounted shadow
strung lots to service them.

I am the center.
My dear party, brothers,
nowhere.

Bodies are lying. Now here. The man in the wheelchair denying terror, overwrought blackening under a rule of blunders. Coarse or amass. Today everyone is sent home which means they create more wrongs than they heal. And he won't leave, who may be heard, stacked stunts in time, as if with lullaby alas.

Those without property will die.
Corporately,
we boot up orgasms.

Golden goofs
downlit
Tog separate skins

Clearing fire. Under a heavy burden, move. Questionless rigor will die sooner, wearing thin, soiled, *to work for him*. Draining sleep who is also but can't tell, distracted, changed feathers, separating gold for a crime. Indifferently arranged, watching time, subject to space, brutal impacted uncouth queue. Her hands below the photo of a pockmarked daughter extrude, they take tanks.

Dying,
which will not stop.

Tender

bent neck

inapprehensible

The room expands when I tell her to go. The words are wrong.

Set to a landscape of sweetheart homes, confessed plot, colored lights, grill and dive. She wants, as in war, to borrow the salesman, but can't tell if attention will hurt. *You count on it.* As in a topic dissent sustained by civilian insouciance, opportune. To lay hold of fear, to enter "undomiciled." The attraction between them is measured by goods she can carry. So carefully handed, the attraction embeds, needing a stricture to go on.

This is the trailer of their hearts,

so even food hurts.

on the lip
of what wasn't
enchantment, contrivance

Votes took place scraping the swaggering sun struck soil. But this was impossible. Censorship not our priority. Equally trounced—tense thing dependent heart. Momentarily revive the upright structure while protocols obliterate the production and copulation explains why she agrees to pose nude six months pregnant. Ostensibly, an ablution of the consultant montage. In front of ourselves a bodily competence. *It was just a battle that I'm sorry to say I lost.* Doom palm fire job. Another point: Who is harassing the question? *I'm no longer part of this world.*

Unconvinced
tanks veil their bodies with manly color
a city gets used to

an inadequate qualm

brutal

light spar

And by Sunday we asked—What had happened? What form the class struggle might take. Protest marking the spots. *For sure* turned into tragedy: *I was a grunting, voracious pig in heat.* Retributive bodies of blue forfeit property—public, yet terminal, fuzzy, stinking, affordable & monthly. *I thought why not open a rat restaurant?* This surgical operation refines greed, rehabbing the neighborhood until enclitic maniacal light eviscerates the end of the story.

To think
in the "land of the free" insures displacement

thereby getting everyone else off

the future
as topic caricature
condemns instance

I'm not saying it didn't happen. We were a fact in each others'
lives. We were brothers, killing (over the top), looking out windows they watch like the rich at a war before we were evidence. The blind faith of freely associated producers spread in perpetual stupor, leaning on taken (beat by), based on

a crucial indifference.

The policewoman has an overriding sense of a different topology.

Without privilege of bed or monopoly
identity skirts focus
Coercive pall

Definition engine, optical enzyme, to make good, fasten. Untempered by solipsism, bolster the idea that this is sufficiently important to deserve your syntax

In which language is not only an expressive embarrassment but a consideration of detail.

atheist bully
bombs tribute
fondle

Dear one lover—In the video people, every family in red white sterility radius. Dirt having beat fire and not broken up the difference you have in mind. Cordon continues poised to make sweep summary justice. Angle on motor. Motor drag of common hate. Officers stand waiting for dawn. The end planned in a protocol of parts. Free products of special angers, most likely machine fists, choking foot of counter-denunciation. Sent home behind barricades according to: *Take it down. Is yours*—linchpin of profit blot. Justifying possession. No name on it. Omit. To grasp at this, clinging to a dysfunctional causality which imitates the day in a logic I deny. I lie yet live in indignity's draft

registering the transgression normality sustains.

under fire

sleep broken

too scared to rule

Poxy blot become System home system message quell and you can't *unsayable* of the design stood still. The police have nothing but orders. To take over brain closes, face does not recognize, diffuse lack, your neighbor, same that takes you away in an apocalypse of machine parts. Protocol made up to make *you*. *You* are the target—allied to begin. Unaccommodated flesh. Bulk riot. Under a promise, have been shyly, watered in plurals to frame a front of seme instability (sun on my left) perpetual and on my right a series of moves, more raw, in that order, not necessarily, meanings happen even if I pull the plug on noise to give delight

causing preposterous

exactitude

in face of cant

variant

cast

Mobilizing the rest in a major paradigm shift. Matrixed figure speaks backwards: alien special in effect, a dream. Efficient deceptions transform your options. Abandon, as when they laugh where she cites crime. Presumptive backdrop stalls our echo. Stricter frag appals. Resists. Interruption swells, full or heroine—a celestial derelict under drag of molecular standing lip. Lie down or in place array nakedness—proof our example. In her argument to make closer bodies electrically charged, our projects hazard theory contradicting parts. No tune to nick, fed verb remembers, arresting sidewalk (divvying it up).
To pull down the block in a public flush

You walk out—

inside the person unsubstantiated

groundwork's condition

BEYOND SURPLUS

for Diane Ward & Andrew Levy

grips legs panties girls
baby doll-ups
too fully on my funny run

kissing a connection
with her hand in a pocket
kissing a and otherwise

waving shaped shape
whispers me up
refused to tell

Relax *psychosound*
1) find another definition NOT based on lack
2) suck suck suck

unmistakable juice and smell and hair
innocently 'sweetheart' clit scream breath blue
thighs hot swollen fully

Look has abundance
Lying played pulled cooed and fatted
focused

suddenly dry
kiss me fuck you
returning real charm

                                        IF I WERE

ATTIRED IN ANY ACCURACY

                                  MY

GARMENTS WOULD FALL STRIDENTLY

                                  INTO ME

Fantasy bends it out of shape
twists in my face
not a nice ass but
a great heart-shaped ledge butt
the bottom
what's written out
an unassimilable

Sit on my face

This pleasure applies to the infant, the masochist,
and the film spectator

Then she pushes me off
head her on her a while
like this idea has me sit next to her

where I'd left my mouth
still horny start again
and got rocking now
gave it to her

I left my pant and put back my mouth
to sit on it to get shirt
pulling time trouble to buck
pushed easily by now
started to suck
to get you

BETWEEN MY THIGHS

YOUR MOUTH IMPROVISING

Following that line of thought
power verbs shape faces on your own
prism cunt
The civilization of the ass unseals
becomes like you when you come
and wear the kind of smile I want to take home

HOW TO TRANSLATE WHAT CANNOT CLOSE

FULL OF HOT and chronic satisfaction
soaked
'cause I'm stopped
between love and a third tongue
girlfriend   sexy buttons   popping cock
twisted   I'm visualizing them physically
the unreasonableness of the situation

                          THIS WORLD

Love mixed with other colors
so big so blonde so full so fill me up

This is your life: *erotic error*
kissing my impeccable cunt

                        PRESSING
HARD,
THE DEPICTION OF MANY ANGLES IN WHICH
                        INVOLVEMENT
                        LINGERS

                        STARE AT
                        LURE

WHAT YOU'VE CREATED IS STRICTLY LIMIT

There's a tangle of questions all over the floor

Shadows tip the lover onto the circumstance
She wants to be touched or touched continuously
The sun makes close enough open
Skirt a retinue of clings
A sanitized restraint gives way
to lustre's substrate

Waiting become an exciting chance to breathe

WE WISHED WE WEREN'T TRUE AND TRIED TO BE
DECONSUMED

This body shadows opacity of desire and then,
the hot sense of it could be coerced

SPEED

MARKED BY DURATIONS

BODIES

CRAMMED NARROW IN THE NIGHT OF

his definition become proscriptive

I want to drink the theory
wilting the interim

Two women get to the bottom of this
The bottom loves to play
throbbing instance of fresh

OUR HEADS
ARE EQUIDISTANT OVER OUR HEELS

Take yourself out

SKETCH AN

OBLITERATION

SURMOUNT

THE FRAME FACE TO FACE

practically every possible way a body could be aroused

Your attention holds up—laughs
What excites me about her? What excites her about me?
All that will contained in this tiny tiny
magazine

Muscles happily
too big just too big
on top of it all
nude and fresh
perverse shape
of the unexpected
of this ass
that crotch
nipple to nipple
arm to arm
undone
I twist
bend over the body

RESULTS IN

AN ORIGIN

NO HANDS OFF

FROM WHERE WE ARE

LEGACY

Chapter 1

No women appear in the composition and no traces of constructive activity can be discerned. It was a dramatic moment. He went to sleep in the precinct suffering from stone. But how does it develop

from one to another? There is no central chamber, no one corridor from which all others debouch. In truth, what looks like the camaraderie of a peaceable kingdom is chiefly due to common fear

and common fatigue. It cannot and need not wholly exorcise it. The root of the word is in Greek meaning "a throw", and the original sense was of throwing normally separate things together. Now, let us

return to the surface of the water. The two women who in any orthodox Bacchanal should be tripping, riotous maenads sedately lead a satyr baby by the hand and carry a big kettle. There are some

cautions to be added to this. The polyphonic siren of Dove has usually four circles of 8, 10, 12 and 16 holes respectively. But if both holes are open at the same time, something else happens. Imagine

a trap door that opens under your feet with absurd suddenness, and a lyrical gust that sweeps you up and then lets you fall with a bump into the next traphole. It is not causal; there is no complete causal determination of the future on the basis of available knowledge of the present. Let us first look at the word itself. In addition to homosexuality—his childhood, his traumas, and his

deprivations were also subjects I did not want to hear about. He replied by turning himself into a stallion, and in that form caught her. History has at last done justice to the memory of this woman,

whose long yellow hair was so beautiful, and whose character was so colorless. It was known to medical writers as a pathological condition. Then there is the school of meteorological interpreters

who regard wind, weather and colors of the skies as the essence of myth. He is something more, just as the background is not mere burlesque. More would not give it. To all these questions

the answers would turn out to be "no." The reasons for not using the London allegory as companion piece to the *Innocent* tapestry can only be conjectured. I decided on a whim to ask about her tattoos.

The answer, an elm. On the other hand, footings were frequently built in a mixed or haphazard bond. They no longer have the charm of the Thirds. Most of these bandits were naturally

courteous, had a native dignity and were by no means unintelligent. The rifle, then, and cunning.

Chapter 2.

Every natural object or phenomenon is charged.

When I stay with her in the day room of the discipline unit, she refuses to speak. There are a variety of reasons, the most obvious being that artifacts never had a life of their own and therefore they cannot be expected to live now. She did not wear one.

While the fire was still spreading, the police arrested a young Dutch Communist, Maria van Lebbe, who was found in the deserted building. We go in and out; even the most assiduous of us is not bound to this vast structure.

This was legality in practice. Slaves, however, convey a more specific meaning. She will say "A fish has bitten me." And then the wire. That subject I have already treated.

He would go on till the last possible minute of course, but if Valentine did not come?

But that is the whole point. The individual event, the act goes far beyond the general law. Such is the personal equation implicit in this one poem.

Chapter 3

The eve of a new production is hardly time to breathe.
Light profiles set out
again
st a background of dark, gray clouds
fantastic
trees reaching far and high into the sky; the dim twilight of
impenetrable forest; the
bluish haze
above
tepid waters; and the strong sunlight
suffusing open landscapes. These were
phenomena.

The six maidens show no amorous excitement whatsoever.

What had happened, of course, was a miracle of integration. My number I remember was 387. The metal was generally brownish, turned black in the ground, and decayed rapidly into a sugarlike consistency. Those men could dream; they could not rule.

We hold the word in mental suspense, as it were, and only visualize in necessity. She was now sitting with her long hair hanging down on both sides of her face in the dejected pose of a sinner in some old picture. Even this behavior was not all bad; it was her attempt to prove she is a woman.

Flaccid soft walls, in any passage with sonorous masses of air, are generally prejudicial to the force of the vibrations.

I never went back to the factory to find out what happened.

Chapter 5

In the experiments, the uppermost plate of the bellows is violently agitated for the deep tones, and when I lay on it, my whole head was set into such powerful sympathetic vibrations that the holes of the rotating disc which vanish

    to an eye at rest
    become again
    separately visible.

    As to scale
    it is scale
    that determines the possibility of detection.

    From this point of view
    the border
    becomes fluid.

    This
    means struggle. There is a real moon
    and a view of the lake instead of a backdrop.

    But the fact is impossible.
    This was a solution by way of subjective
    deliverance.

    At Ventura, status is gained
    by cooperating with the program, not
    by defying it.

The directive
in discussing the consequences of
Russia's industrial population noted:

Many tens of millions of people
will become redundant.
None.

Most of *you* know what it means
when a hundred corpses are lying side by
side, or five hundred or one thousand.

Chapter 4 contains a comparison: —moans that perhaps are those of an imposter.

Were the waves an illusion, after all?

(This monogrammatic
        interconnection
of two
                individual
        brain patterns
        is not unknown
        in
        so-
        called
        real
        life.)

But I know what I'd do. I'd get more. It may be stupid, but that's how it is.

In other words, the rat conceives nothing less than a genuine five-year plan!

Would the magnitude of the fear that had found expression in this built space allow them to use it in ways just as uncontrolled and insane—thinking it authorized them somehow?

I do not mean this at all contemptuously.

Whenever light acts on matter or is produced by it we find packets of defined energy and impulse related to the quantum of action.

I am dubious

The plain fact about democracy is that it is a physical impossibility.

My own state of mind synthesizes these two feelings and transcends them: my mind is pessimistic, but my will is optimistic.

She's little but I tell you she's a whizzer.

This inclination in creatures not endowed with cognition is called natural desire. Now we are ready for the two dreams

A year later.

I needed a few days more to get rid of my smile, which seemed stereotyped like a ballerina's.

(Prose): *You broke the bridges?*

In the semidarkness I climbed over mountains of trunks and little hills of perambulators, got hung in a chain, and suffered from unspeakable smells, and at last was ordered upstairs again. The first unsplit instant in my life.

(Instant): *I don't want anything to grow too big for me; even though I may want to experience it.*

The bigger the unit you deal with, the hollower, the more brutal, the more mendacious is the life displayed.
Just to sell.

Why is this tendency "characteristic"?

In so far as they are administered! Charming people who meant so much to us in the nineties have vanished from our horizon.

I want a hundred housefuls of it!

What counts are the impressions before the subject. Thereafter the fibers ran lengthwise. *You bet.* Photography was invented at the right moment as a warning against materialistic vision.

They were down in the Cold War dream,
the voices fading
from the radios,
the unwatchable events in the sky,
the flight,
the long descent,
the escape to refuge deep in earth,
one hatchway after another,
leading to smaller and smaller volumes.

All this is more likely. The consumer has to invent her own images, and it is felt, I do not know with what justification, that there is no harm in this.

(A tender hug.) She decides to act.

Chapter 7

All well and good, but how? Does the whole composition have a discernible pla
n
a sense of control
led and directed motion
from point A to B to   X,   Y   and
    Z?

She sums up her aims thus:

>*I propose to set up the life in common*

Movies and television have made this street familiar.

His hint of the economic failure of communism is not as convincing as his revelation of the basic fallacy in the proposal to establish a community of women. When I came home I felt rather like Cinderella where the chariot and horses revert to pumpkin and mice.

In most countries an abyss separates what you see
and what you don't
see,
but the abyss here
is deeper
than in any other civilized country.

Nobody mentions her, although the subject dies more slowly.

There was plenty of flak from that.

>*I have had enough.*

We should look for nothing less.

To emphasize the beautiful seems to me like a mathematical system that only concerns itself with positive numbers.

RAPTURE

Backhanded industrials give mathematical evidence of
control.
We judge the method of manufacture from structural whites.
Gut-shot suckers freely, spits moisture lilies. Against
the overeaten sun, there's pumping

Parades smell thickly in form a resolute and voluminous
tactic lies forgot. A swell tune. Yet needing to function,
I capitulate. I cannot control the full participation
of your alerts.

Weather testifies to pressure you pull off. The sun tears up
the window. Agains ceiling clouds climb. Time
replaces sequence—beat in front of drama. The first place
of meaning

include a color calmer, a proto integrator, a liquid straight a
maze. Space footlights this transference. In love,
the light upcoming, rising open mocked across
night, unrepeatable and not

entirely fictive. Bright leaves forfeit nostalgia, print
pandemonium on a permeable plural.

Other O Books

Return of the World, Todd Baron, $6.50
A Certain Slant of Sunlight, Ted Berrigan, $9.00
Talking in Tranquility: Interviews with Ted Berrigan, Avenue B and O Books, $10.50
Mob, Abigail Child, $9.50
It Then, Danielle Collobert, $9.00
Candor, Alan Davies, $9.00
Turn Left in Order to Go Right, Norman Fischer, $9.00
Precisely the Point Being Made, Norman Fischer, Chax Press and O Books, $10.00
Time Rations, Benjamin Friedlander, $7.50
byt, William Fuller, $7.50
The Sugar Borders, William Fuller, $9.00
Phantom Anthems, Robert Grenier, $6.50
What I Believe Transpiration/Transpiring Minnesota, Robert Grenier, $24.00
The Inveterate Life, Jessica Grim, $7.50
A Memory Play, Carla Harryman, $9.50
The Quietist, Fanny Howe, $9.00
Values Chauffeur You, Andrew Levy, $9.00
Dreaming Close By, Rick London, $5.00
Abjections, Rick London, $3.50
Dissuasion Crowds the Slow Worker, Lori Lubeski, $6.50
Catenary Odes, Ted Pearson, $5.00
(where late the sweet) BIRDS SANG, Stephen Ratcliffe, $8.00
Visible Shivers, Tom Raworth, $8.00
Kismet, Pat Reed, $8.00
Cold Heaven, Camille Roy, $9.00
O ONE/AN ANTHOLOGY, ed. Leslie Scalapino, $10.50
O TWO/AN ANTHOLOGY: What is the inside, what is outside? What is censoring? What is being censored?, ed. Leslie Scalapino, $10.50
O/3: WAR, ed. Leslie Scalapino, $4.00
O/4: Subliminal Time, ed. Leslie Scalapino, $10.50
Crowd and not evening or light, Leslie Scalapino, Sun & Moon and O Books, $9.00
The India Book: Essays and Translations, Andrew Schelling, $9.00
A's Dream, Aaron Shurin, $8.00
Picture of The Picture of The Image in The Glass, Craig Watson, $8.00
Collision Center, Randall Potts, $9.00